Seasons

of

Discovery

52 Weeks of Intentional Change

By

Edward Stratton

ISBN: 9781983317453

FIRST EDITION

Printed in the United States of America

Interior Formatting by

Deadly Reads Author Services

Cover Design by

David Green

TABLE OF CONTENTS

SEASON FOUR: WINTER

CONCLUSION

P.S. (Just one more thing...)

About the Author

Acknowledgements

FOREWORD

I had the pleasure of meeting Eddie in the mid-nineties when he was beginning his spiritual journey. I soon became his friend and teacher. As anyone who watches their students grow, I have immense pride in the person that he has become. This book is the accumulation of his desire to grow and to share what he has learned in the process. I am proud to say that the student has become the teacher.

Seasons of Discovery is a jewel of a book that features a new lesson every week for a total of 52 weeks. Each lesson is filled with gentle guidance, to assist you toward living a more rewarding life. The tasks are not difficult, yet you must be willing to go within and embrace the real you. Eddie's wisdom will nudge you in the right direction. Seasons of Discovery not only asks you to think about yourself, but gives concrete, yet simple ways to move forward and take charge of your life. Each week offers the opportunity to grow towards a more fulfilling life.

Regardless of where you are on your spiritual journey, each lesson is a reminder to focus on our desires and to live the best life possible. I found it inspirational and a reminder that we all have work to do to become the person we deserve to be.

If you are ready for a change, open the page and begin a journey to wholeness. You will be amazed at the end of the 52 weeks at how much you have grown.

Dee Patterson Pusey

Professional Psychic & Medium

Spiritual Teacher

INTRODUCTION

Dear Reader,

The journey you are about to embark on in the pages and exercises that follow will help to assist you in creating a better life and a much better you. Let me begin by saying, YOU are responsible for your life! The keys to your happiness are in your pocket, no one else's. In taking responsibility for our lives, we are given the opportunity to make our lives what we want them to be. We can be the change that is needed, or we can stay stuck in the place where we have always been. It is truly up to us to create the life that we want to see. We must trust the process of life and know that like seasons, our life will have many changes, beginnings and completions. We must learn to let go of what no longer serves us if we are to become who we wish to be. One of the biggest tools of understanding is that Life happens FOR and not TO us. Everything is for our personal growth and evolution.

In the weekly entries that follow, I offer opportunities of learning, self-examination and a hope that you can manifest the things that you desire. I refer to a "Higher Source" often throughout this book as a means of reference to the belief in something greater than ourselves. What you wish to call this "Source" is up to you. I believe in a power that is greater than me and I call on it often to help, assist and guide me in manifesting and directing the path that I wish to follow. I use and close each entry with the help of an affirmation.

Affirmations are short and supportive statements that help to give power and direction to the things that we wish to see in life. It is important in using them that we make them statements of power, belief, trust and knowing that all things are with us and possible. Use them as tools to pull to you your heart's desires and remember to make them in the "present tense," so that they have the power to be with you now and not in some distant time. Affirmations also help us to let go of the things that need to leave our life and to give us acceptance and trust that all we need will be given. All is possible!

This book is laid out according to the seasonal changes that happen in nature. I believe that process is a great metaphor of how our lives flow. When something ends, something new begins. We let go of the old to make way for the new. In this book, I hope that you will find the tools helpful or necessary to manifest a new and perfect you and life. If we are to bring about the changes that we wish to see, we must change. We cannot always play it safe. We must be brave and daring to take the leaps of faith that are needed if we are to obtain the life that we wish to see. Taking a leap can be a scary thing, but we grow our faith muscles when we do. We learn to trust that we can be powerful beings who are meant to achieve greater things.

Let me remind you that you do not have to stay where you have always been. You have the choice and the right to create the life that you want to see. It begins with a thought and a dream that it is possible and with a passion to make it happen. We don't always need to know where we are going or what the outcome will be, but we can trust the journey and know that where we end up will be better than where we have been.

My wish for you is that you consider the lessons presented to you in this book and that you have a willingness to carefully examine the parts of you that need acknowledgement of what keeps you from having a better life. We are all deserving of the very best that life has to offer. It is up to us to claim it! I want to bring out your best and to let you know that YOU MATTER! Your life matters and the dreams and visions that you have for your life are possible; they matter. I hope that you use this book to remind you of your greatness. Do the work on the themes and pages that follow and be completely honest with yourself where needed.

I wish you the best in manifesting the desires of your heart. Let the manifesting begin, let the discoveries of you unfold. I wish you every happiness. Good luck on your journey!

Peace and love,

Eddie

Spring

IMAGINE

Imagine if you will, living your wildest dreams. Can you imagine what that would feel like? Can you see yourself doing what you love and living the life that you want? The job, the money, the house, the partner or car, all the things that you desire? It can happen. Here's the thing: They are waiting on you! How?

First, they must start in your mind and next, in your heart and then are followed by the knowledge that you can have them. What you are looking for is looking for you. We are all energy and "like attracts like." We pull to us the people, places and things that we give focus to.

What are your belief systems? Do you know? Do you trust others? Do you believe that people are out to get you? Do you believe that you don't deserve to be paid what you are worth? Do you live with a "lack" mentality? Your underlying belief systems are the subconscious thoughts that we think and project. If we don't monitor them properly, they give power to things that we manifest into our lives. Every thought that we think is like a silent prayer, so examine what you believe carefully and know that a thought can be changed. I bring up your belief system because I want you to be able to manifest the things that you imagine. We must remember that thoughts are things and the negative ones can cancel out the positive things that we want to create.

This week deeply explore your beliefs and what you give your attention to. What thoughts do you need to change? Then, imagine what you want to bring into your life. Make a list and describe each one perfectly. Next, imagine yourself in the present moment with each one. Imagine what it would be like to have them in your possession. Remember, imagination is the seed in which things grow. Imagine and on the page ahead, dream your wildest dreams and know that you can have what your heart desires. The heart gets what the heart wants!

Weekly Affirmation:

I deserve the very best that life and love have to offer! I dream what I want into existence, easily and effortlessly.

My Thoughts

MEDITATION

Last week, we started focusing on the power of intention. This week we begin with taking time to meditate. Meditation is valuable in manifesting the things that we desire. It provides the insights that we need to understand our daily lives. Meditation is like watering the soil for our seeds to grow. Meditation practice allows us the ability to see ourselves with the things that we want to create. It also gives us the steps needed to achieve our heart's desires.

Meditation is like the muscles of the body; it must be developed to grow stronger. How will we ever hear, if we never listen? We need to take a few moments every day to stop, breathe and hear the things that our lives are trying to tell us or show us. Our life whispers to us constantly and through the practice of meditation, we can hear what we need to know.

Meditation comes in varied forms. There is no one right way; do whatever works for you. It is the ability to shut out the world around you and to go within and listen. Meditation can be done with soft music, low lighting and candles, but it can also be done while walking in nature, listening to music, daydreaming, bathing, exercising, or through journaling. I believe meditation is a useful tool to co-creating with the Universe the life that we dream of living. If nothing else, it gives us a chance to give back to ourselves and to explore the depths of self.

This week take the time to stop(!), breathe and listen to what your life is trying to show you. When we are busy in our life, we can't hear. Take at least five minutes daily to practice this insightful art and write down your experiences and feelings.

Weekly Affirmation:

I trust myself to know the things that I need to know. Everything that I need to know is NOW being revealed to me. I relax in this knowing.

My Thoughts

_____

_____

_____

_____

_____

_____

_____

_____

_____

_____

_____

_____

_____

_____

_____

THE EGG

The Egg is the starting point, the beginning, and it symbolizes birth. The idea (intention), must first be seeded. What do you want to manifest? To see it in the outside world, you must first believe it! That's right, you will see it when you believe it. So, your Egg must be the seed that you plant and much like a plant, it will need daily watering to bring it forth.

How do we do that? Through choosing a ritual that best works for you. One that can be done easily and effortlessly, that allows you to focus on your desire. What is a ritual? It is the practice of repeated affirming on which focus is given to the thing(s) that you are celebrating. An affirmation is a great way to practice a ritual. An affirmation is a short, clear statement declaring power over a thing. The shorter and clearer the statement, the easier it is to repeat and the more likely you will be to able to say it, do it, repeat it several times a day and to believe it.

Also, keep affirmations in the NOW! We want to see what we desire with us now, in this present moment, not kept in the future. Once you get the hang of writing and coming up with affirmations, the more fun you will have and the easier they are to do. You will find that your Egg, no matter how small the desire, will be easier with a powerful affirmation. The Egg could be something simple like creating a great parking space. The affirmation could be, "I now create the right and perfect parking space for me!" or, "A close and handy place to park is now being made possible for me!" Did you notice that I made them simple and used the term NOW to make it present and to give it power? So, whatever it is, start this week with playing with your new friend, Affirmation. She is waiting to help and assist you. In the page ahead, jot down your experimentations using affirmations and see how they work for you.

Weekly Affirmation:

Everything I need is now available for me. All is in perfect timing.

My Thoughts

_____

_____

_____

_____

_____

_____

_____

_____

_____

_____

_____

_____

_____

PASSION

What ignites your passion? What sets you on fire? What do you want more than anything? Whatever it is, that is your passion. Does it make you feel alive, or does it frighten you? You cannot really have the thing (or things), that excites you without passion. I once heard it said that your passion is what gets you out of bed in the morning. Your passion is your heart's desire. It is the ultimate love story. The more that you want it, the more that it consumes you, and the more that it consumes you, the more likely you are to have it with you.

The word Desire means to want or to hope for something. The word Passion means a strong feeling of enthusiasm or excitement for something. So, desire and passion go hand in hand. Passion and desire will help to bring to you the thing, or things that you want in your life.

What can you do this week to spark passion into your life? What steps can you take to show to the Universe that you mean business when it comes to manifesting what you want into your life? Even if they are small steps, it still shows your intention towards bringing what you want into your life.

Describe your passion and what it would feel like to have it with you now. Remember, you can have the very things that you crave.

Weekly Affirmation:

I **AM** passionate about_____ and I bring it into my life with ease and excitement.

My Thoughts

_____

_____

_____

_____

_____

_____

_____

_____

_____

_____

_____

_____

_____

ACTING AS IF

We have all heard the phrase, "Fake it until you make it," but have you ever thought about what that means? It means that you pretend to be doing something that you love, that you are enjoying what you are doing. In the field of creative visualization, we "act as if" or "pretend" that the things that we want are already in our possession. When we talk about them, we should describe them with detail and speak of them "as if" we already have them in our life.

When we were children, we played with great imagination, as if the idea that we were playing with was in our grubby little hands. We need that same intensity to bring more of the good into our life.

We spend so much of our time focusing on the wrong things, like lack, or what we don't have and guess what? What we focus on, we create. So, what we focus on, becomes our intention. We need to get our focus muscles back into shape and concentrate on developing the things we want, versus the things that we don't have. Acting as if, sets the wheels in motion for bringing more abundance into the picture. The more that we pretend to have our heart's desire, the more that we increase it being with us, if we are meant to have it.

Refueling the fire... What you want is waiting on you to take that first step. This week, will you "act as if" and begin the mission of pulling the very best to you? In the space provided, what or how can you fake it until you make it?

Weekly Affirmation:

I love having _____! It has brought so much joy and happiness to my life.

My Thoughts

_____

_____

_____

_____

_____

_____

_____

_____

_____

_____

_____

_____

_____

_____

FLEXIBILITY

With our focus on intention comes the need to remain open and flexible. We have done the work, followed the steps, practiced the faith and trust, but things seem to not be happening or going according to our plan. We must remain flexible, knowing that what is meant for us will find us. We must remain flexible in the understanding that we will not always get what we want. We must stay flexible believing that there is a plan. We must know that what looks like a delay or a rejection, is merely a re-direction that will lead us to our best destination.

Staying flexible means bending, going with the flow, trusting the steps towards our highest good and the highest good of all involved, keeping an open mind and yet, remaining strong and moldable. Trust and surrender this process and know that all is well. When we release our control and let the Universe guide our desires, we will find our lives more richly blessed in divine possibilities.

This week examine the areas where you have trouble being flexible. Do you trust? Do you practice faith? Do you believe that you truly deserve the things you say that you want? Examine these questions and write down your answers.

Weekly Affirmation:

I am flexible! I keep an open mind, trusting that what is meant for me will find me. All is well.

My Thoughts

_____

_____

_____

_____

_____

_____

_____

_____

_____

_____

_____

_____

_____

_____

FOUNDATION

What creates a good foundation? In visualizing your future dreams, a solid foundation is built with your thoughts and beliefs. Every thought that we think, is creating the world in which we see. What we focus on is creating the foundation that our thoughts are producing. That is why it is imperative to keep your thoughts only on "the good" and know and trust that everything is happening as it should; that all will be revealed when the time is right.

The building blocks that are your foundation are falling into place, even when you cannot see any results. Keep going! Do not pull out in the middle of what you are doing just because it seems that you are going nowhere. Do not stop before the miracle has arrived. Every good builder knows the importance of a good, solid foundation. Without proper footing and preparation, the structure will not be stable and will not yield a good result. So, the beginning of your dream is very important. The beginning thoughts that you have and keep will either make or break your creation. Keep your focus only on the desire that you can achieve what it is that you want to create.

This week, if needed, re-examine your thoughts and beliefs. Ask yourself, are you staying true to who you are? Do you believe that you deserve to have what you desire? Get rid of all self-doubt or self-defeating beliefs that are sabotaging your outcome. The thing(s) that you are trying to bring to you will only come... if **YOU BELIEVE!** Your belief is your foundation.

Weekly Affirmation:

Every thought that I think is creating my future. I am worthy of every good thing. I trust and believe that all I desire is now coming to me when the time is right.

My Thoughts

WHISPERING

Life constantly whispers to us. Are you listening? There is a gentle flow and rhythm to life. It is like a sweet and soft melody that is playing in the background of our life. It is helping to direct us in our life decisions and it is there to help guide us along the journey of life.

When we fail to listen to this rhythm, our life does not go as planned. It is like a small stone that causes a great ripple effect when left unnoticed. It is our responsibility to notice the subtle effects of our lives and to not let the small stone turn into the brick wall that comes tumbling down on top of us. We must stop and listen to our lives. How will we ever hear if we don't tune out the world, our lives, and listen for our answers? Answers cannot get in if we are living in or are caught up in chaos and drama.

Our subtle messages come in many forms such as dreams, music, art, writing, reading, meditation, signs, bumper stickers, billboards, etc. It is up to us to pay attention and LISTEN to what the Universe is trying to show us. Once we ask for what we want, WE must get out of our own way and let the Universe take the lead.

This week take the time to get quiet, really quiet and listen to what your life is trying to show you. Ask for what you need to know to be revealed to you so you do not pass it by when it arrives. Stay alert and attuned to your life and the whisper that it is trying to speak to you. Can you hear it? You will, if you listen.

Weekly Affirmation:

I now hear the subtle messages of life. I am in the flow of life and it leads me to the right and perfect destination for me. Only the best comes to me now. I am aware!

My Thoughts

_____

_____

_____

_____

_____

_____

_____

_____

_____

_____

_____

_____

_____

OTHERS

In life, we seek the opinion of others. This can be a good thing, but it can also be a bad thing. When we are trying to build the blueprint of our life, we need to be careful what we share with others. When we share our deepest secrets, we are creating an opening for others to speak their judgment and criticism, so we need to be careful with whom we share our secrets.

There is a small quiet voice that runs through each of us. It is the gift of knowing. We all have it. It is our own internal GPS, so to speak. It is there to help guide and direct us throughout our daily life. If we learn to listen to it, we can hear what is best for us. When we listen to this subtle voice, we will find and discover that outside validation is not needed. You know what you know! If the voice is loud, fearful, or shaky, it is not the correct voice to listen to—that is fear. The voice of God, the Universe, whatever you wish to call it, is calm and peaceful, that is the instinct to follow.

Others can be helpful and their intentions good, but they can also hold us back and keep us from manifesting what is best for us. Remember, just because someone smiles at you, does not mean that they are your friend. Your dreams and visions matter to you and sometimes, things are meant to be kept private until further notice.

This week, work on turning within and hearing your own voice of reason. The saying is true: "Follow your heart. It will never lead you wrong."

Weekly Affirmation:

I now trust my own inner voice. All that I need to know resides within me. I honor and trust myself. I am constantly led in the right direction.

My Thoughts

HIGHER POWER

There is a higher power at work in our lives. It is there to help and assist us whenever needed. This Source doesn't care what you call it; it just wants us to acknowledge them and to ask for their assistance. This Higher Power reminds us that we are never alone and that we do not have to handle things on our own. It is there to help love, guide and support us in all that we need. This Higher Power is love, peace, joy, happiness, support, comfort and most of all strength, to help carry us through our challenges and disappointments. Source waits for us to ask for help and then for us to step out of our own way and let them bring to us the things that are best for us. It is true, we may not always get what we want, but we always get what we need. That is the power behind this source. It is always there, silently and gracefully waiting to assist us in our daily needs.

Have you tapped into your Source? Do you have a daily conversation or acknowledgement with them? Do you truly let go and offer up to IT the things of your heart? Do you believe, most importantly, in a force that is higher than yourself?

This week check in with your Higher Source. Ask IT to support and love you. Ask IT to make you aware of their presence. Surrender to them your hopes and dreams and then, trust that the good that you deserve will come to you, at all times and in THEIR time and order.

Weekly Affirmation:

I now trust in The Divine, to lead and to guide my way. I surrender and allow this Source to bring to me now all that I hope for and what is truly best for me. All is well in my world.

My Thoughts

GRATITUDE

Gratitude is the ultimate in expression. Where would we be without it? Not very far. The best thing that we can ever do is to say thank you! We should make it a daily ritual to give thanks and praise for all that we have. It takes such little effort and yields such high results.

When we give thanks and show our deepest gratitude, it unleashes more to come into our lives. Every time that we receive, especially the things that we have prayed, manifested and asked for, we should stop and offer our deepest thanks for all that we have been given. Even when we are not trying to manifest and ask for things, we should just say thank you. Each morning before getting out of bed, we should make it a practice to say thank you for this day. A new day is a gift. Life is a gift. Breathing and walking, seeing and hearing, are all gifts that we take for granted. So, with that said, we have so much to be grateful for, not just when we receive something.

This week, can you begin and end your day with gratitude? Take the time to express all that you are thankful for and as you move throughout your day, remember to thank the Universe for all that you have and all that you receive. The famous quote from Meister Eckhart is true, "If the only prayer that you ever say in your entire life is thank you, it will be enough."

Weekly Affirmation:

I am so very thankful for all that I have, all that I give, and for all that I receive. I am now truly blessed.

My Thoughts

ENDINGS, COMPLETIONS AND RESURRECTION

They say in life that "All good things must end." When the time has come for an ending to take place, the season as we have known it must end. In life, some things need to die away for new things to grow. We have all heard the phrase "When one door closes another one will open" and that is true when the endings of life are upon us.

Endings are not necessarily a bad thing. It just means that a new time is upon us and even when it does not feel like it, a new dawn is coming. Remember, the right person, place or thing cannot come into our life if the wrong thing or person is blocking the way.

I have discovered in my own life as I do self-reflection, how many times that I have died "mini-deaths" only to be re-born. These so called, "mini-deaths" were needed to help me shed the parts of myself that needed to be let go of. As painful as they were, I needed them to happen to become who I am today. The old things must die away so new things can be born.

Like the Christ, we have all been crucified in our own lives. We were judged, persecuted and hanged in order to learn about survival, forgiveness, mercy and salvation, that something better could be on the way and a new Spirit, called You, could be resurrected.

Where in life have you been crucified or treated unfairly? Can you examine your trials and tribulations and see where change was needed and maybe, just maybe... a new and better way was born? Have you forgiven your past and your transgressors that treated you unfairly, but paved a way for a resurrection to take place in you? It is hard to remember and to hold onto the knowledge that all is happening as it should. Divine time and order are perfectly in place, at all times and in all things. What is meant for us will find us and that change is sometimes needed to move us in the path that is meant for us to follow. All is well.

Weekly Affirmation:

I trust the process of endings and completions in my life. Life knows what is best for me and I trust that only the best will find me. I let go and I let God!

My Thoughts

SURRENDER

Any good farmer knows that after the soil has been properly worked and the seeds planted, Mother Nature now takes the lead. Yes, it is true that he must do his part of carefully watering and attending to his new crop, but the unseen forces of Nature will yield the result.

So, your seeds have been planted and you have wished upon your star, now comes the hard part... the surrender! The toughest part of intentional work is offering it up and letting things happen as they should. Waiting can be difficult. We want things on our time and then, even quicker than that. In our world of smart phones and instant gratification, we expect the Universe to deliver the same way. I am sorry to say that it doesn't work that way. There is a season to all things and a perfect time and order under heaven. If we are patient, our harvest will come and will be to our highest interests and our efforts will have paid off.

We try to control everything. Wouldn't it be nice if someone else took the lead and did things for us? Now is that chance. Remember, worry is wasted energy and often, it keeps our hopes and dreams from coming to us.

When we truly surrender and let it go, that is when "IT" comes.

This week, can you let go and trust that what is meant for you will not pass you by? Can you take your hands off the wheel and let the divine guide your way? Surrender and letting go takes courage, practice, faith and a healthy dose of trusting that all is well—that you could even live without your desired object. That's surrender! The total trust that all will be okay, with or without, and the world will not stop revolving. All *IS* well.

Weekly Affirmation:

I let go and I now surrender!

My Thoughts

Summer

THE FUTURE

What do you want your future to look like? Can you describe it with detail? That is your assignment this week, to visualize what you want your life to look like. Do whatever you can to capture it and set it into motion. How can we do that?

You can start by making a list, forming an affirmation that is simple, in the present moment and one that gives it power and authority; you can journal about your hopes and dreams, make a treasure board and use pictures and words to describe it. Lastly... when you talk about it, talk as if it is already with you and how it feels to have it in your life.

The future is in your hands, but you must believe that you can have it. You can have the life that you desire. I encourage you to surrender the past and to live in the present moment, to look to the future with great hope and promise of things to come. When you ask what is coming, say "Only the very best is coming!" We have spent enough time fueling lack into our lives; it is time to focus on creating the good.

This week spend some time and write about your future. What do you want to see? Describe it vividly and in detail, leaving nothing out! Watch your thoughts and beliefs; only give power to what you want to have. Our thoughts and words, whether they are spoken aloud or silently, become our prayers. I believe that the Universe says YES to every request. So, choose what you speak and think carefully. Know that you deserve the very best!

Weekly Affirmation:

I plan my future carefully and in detail! I only plant seeds of good things to come. My future is now happening. I live the life of my dreams and I deserve it!

My Thoughts

SHINE

This week's message comes to remind you of your greatness, to encourage you to keep going and moving in the right direction. I want to remind you that there could be others that want to try to knock you from your path. Don't let them. Your purpose is to follow your passion and to do what is necessary for your life. This is YOUR life! You get to decide what is right and best for you. Throughout your life, you will be presented with tests and it is up to you to take them. No one else will do it for you; no one else can. They are your lessons, so do them, learn from them and most importantly... grow from them.

Others who are afraid to step out of their comfort zones will try to persuade you differently. They will bring their self-defeating reasons of why you should stay where you have always been, to maybe convince you that you cannot do what it is that you want to do, or to sabotage your dreams with fear and judgment. Remember... they are afraid! They are not brave like you are. Like a Vampire, they cannot stand in the light; if they do, they will shrivel up. They must stay in their box of safety and their dreams and goals never happen.

Your challenge is to see and recognize those issues and people when they show up and to not agree with their agenda. Your agenda is to shine your light and to live fearlessly and courageously and to do it better than ever before. Your enemies come to teach you valuable lessons. Find those lessons and show them your determination. Never allow someone to steal your shine!

This week examine where you have allowed others to determine your life. Where have others held you back? Where have others taught you to be afraid and to play it safe? Examine these issues and journal them out. Never let someone else's opinion be your confirmation.

Weekly Affirmation:

I will not let anyone take away my joy! I am following my dream! I will not allow others to dull my shine! I am brave and fearless, and my future is bright!

My Thoughts

CHANGE

Change is never easy, but for us to *have* change, we *must* change. It can be frightening to leave our comfort zones. We tend to get contented in them and we don't realize that we are stuck in them. We stay in places and with people longer than we should because we feel it is safer to stay than to experience the unknown.

Fear is one of our biggest teachers. It keeps us stuck in our lives and yet can be our biggest indicator of what we should be doing. If you were or are like me, I was taught to be afraid of everything! That if I stepped out of "the norm" something terrifying would happen to me. So, throughout my life I played it safe and stayed in my nests that were normal and predictable and most of all, safe. I have learned that the very thing that we fear is what we should be doing. The more that we fear a thing... the more that it is life showing us the direction that we should be moving in.

Fear can be our friend. It is a part of our built-in GPS, our internal navigational system. We must learn how to use it and let it guide us toward our dreams and choices. We need to know how to use our own intuition and learn how to navigate through the choices that present themselves along our way. If something doesn't feel good to us we need to heed that, but if it feels good... we need to bust through the fear.

Change isn't easy. But, if we are to achieve the desires of our heart, we need to make friends with it and use fear to make the changes that we need to make. Franklin D. Roosevelt rightly said, "The only thing we have to fear is fear itself!"

This week, ask yourself: What is it that I am afraid of? List the answers that follow that question and be completely honest. Also, what is it that I fear will happen if I do _____?

Weekly Affirmation:

I am no longer afraid! Fear is my friend and it pushes me along and encourages me to make the right choices for me. I am at peace with fear. I am fearless!!

My Thoughts

_____

_____

_____

_____

_____

_____

_____

_____

_____

_____

_____

_____

_____

_____

PURPOSE

Are you living your purpose? Are you willing to step out and into your greatness? The saying "Many are called, but few are chosen" poses the question, are you willing to answer the calling for your life? Are you willing to be a Leader in your life and show the world who you are and what you are made of? Being a good Leader does carry with it a great deal of responsibility. Are you ready to take that on? To take that next step?

Your purpose is waiting on you, even if you don't know what that is. Be willing to step out of your comfort zone and ask to be shown the way. Willingness to step up will start the journey needed to take you where you wish to go, but it must start with answering the call. Stepping up shows the world that you are secure with yourself and that you mean business.

Your sacred journey is waiting on you! It is time for you to understand that you matter, your life matters and the world needs your power to help to contribute to its goodness. It is time for you to BE what you wish to see! BE the things that you want to see more of in your life. Be a friend, be a smile, a hug, a warm hello, be a bright spot in someone's dark day, be love, be joy, be happiness. Set an intention daily to go into your world and live courageously and be all the things that you wish to see, expecting nothing in return, but knowing that your greatness is making a valuable difference for everyone you come in contact with including yourself. Remember, what you give out is what you WILL receive.

This week, where can you show the world that you mean business? How can you be what you wish to see? Are you willing to be the Leader in your life? How can you demonstrate your abilities? Know your greatness and set forth in your purpose. Be daring and take ownership of your life! Follow your bliss.

Weekly Affirmation:

I am powerful! I courageously live my life with passion and concern, not only for the world in which I live, but for me! I follow my purpose with great passion. I am open to following my heart and know that it leads me to my best life.

My Thoughts

PERMISSION

This week's assignment is easy. I want you to give yourself permission to do what it is that makes you happy. Your bliss is waiting for you to follow it, so do it. That dream needs to be made a reality, do it. We spend so much of our time talking about doing stuff, but we hold back and don't follow through. This week I say, give yourself permission and go for it! The future lies in your hands and the keys to your happiness are in your pocket. So, what are you waiting for?

Give yourself the permission you need and go after your best life. Do it and do it without apologies and let go of the thinking that it is selfish, because I think it is Self-Full! We waste so much of our time putting others first. We have needs also and it is perfectly okay to do what we need to take care of ourselves. Even something as simple as a day off is needed and it is perfectly fine to give yourself permission to do so.

This week, what areas do you need to give yourself "Self-Permission"? What areas can you say, WTH? and go for it? As the Macy Gray song says, "How will we make it, if we never even try?" This week examine the reasons why you hold yourself back and then, work on the reasons that could cause you to fly.

Weekly Affirmation:

I give myself permission to live my best life. I know what is right for me and I give myself permission to follow my dreams and to create the world that works best for me. It is okay for me, to be... ME!

My Thoughts

_____

_____

_____

_____

_____

_____

_____

_____

_____

_____

_____

_____

_____

LOVE

We all want more love. It is the ultimate seeking. We want to experience love from others and we want to feel it for ourselves. They say that the greatest gift that we will ever receive is to love and to be loved in return. We spend so much time obsessing, trying to find it outside of us.

I know that I have spent the greater part of my life wanting someone to love me, looking for someone to make me feel like I was loved, that I mattered, that I was okay. I turned to alcohol and sex and other various empty resources looking for it. They became my drug of choice, but the drug always wore off and I was left feeling broken, empty and more alone. They did become teachers that taught me about self-worth and self-respect. I made it an intention to finally love myself and to know what that could be. I spent years in therapy. I read countless books. I wrote and journaled and took the painful road of looking at my past, re-viewing the images and experiences that first caused my beliefs about love.

What I found is we must be willing to look at ourselves, honestly and completely, and accept us just the way we are and know that we are worthy of love. We are lovable and worth loving. I had to re-learn how to give and receive love, but it had to start with loving me.

This week, how can you be more loving with yourself? How can you forgive yourself and others about your loving experiences? How can you be what you wish to receive? This week offer forgiveness to yourself and begin to offer it to whoever hurt you. It isn't forgiving them for what they did so much as it is setting yourself free from the pain of the experience, so that you can find what you are looking for. Remember, the right one can't get in if the wrong one is blocking the way. And, the greatest love of all is the love that you have with yourself. That's where it must start.

Weekly Affirmation:

I love me! I forgive me! I am worth loving! I am loved and lovable! I forgive myself and all others. I am love and I now am experiencing the love that I deserve!

My Thoughts

_____

_____

_____

_____

_____

_____

_____

_____

_____

_____

_____

_____

_____

REJECTION

This week we are dealing with the possibility of rejection. Rejection isn't easy and it can have devastating consequences—if we let it. But rejection can also be a helpful friend and can help us to navigate through our lives. Sometimes, when we are trying to manifest things, or we are trying to make things happen, we experience setbacks and the dreaded rejection.

I used to take rejection so personally. It made me feel unwanted and like a huge failure. I would let it wound me to the point that I would stop and not pursue my dreams any further. For example, there's someone that you are interested in dating. You ask them out and they reject you and you feel wounded, but then... you find out what a jerk they are. That's rejection looking out for your best interests.

One day, I read a very valuable insight that said, "A rejection is merely a redirection, leading you to a better outcome." I got the message that even though a rejection can be hard to take, someone or something was looking out for my best interests. I have learned that if something is truly meant for me, it will find me. I also have learned that what I am pursuing (whatever it is) should happen easily and effortlessly. If not... it is NOT meant to happen.

It is all about acceptance and perception. If we can shift our perception from failure and rejection to the acceptance of something not being for us, then we understand the meaning of it becoming our friend. Rejection is one of the other internal GPS options that we all have, the great navigating friend and support system that gently (and sometimes abruptly) guides us to our best possible outcome.

This week, work on the acceptance of rejection and how it can help you to determine your best future. How can you relax in the knowledge that what is meant for you will find you? Can you trust that what is coming will be even better than you can even imagine?

Weekly Affirmation:

I now trust and have faith that the Universe is gently guiding and directing me towards my highest and best outcome. I get out of my own way and let my Source do the work. What is truly meant for me now finds me.

My Thoughts

BREATHE

After rejection, it is a good time to stop, take a pause and breathe. When we stop and take a breath, we will be able to listen to our internal self and figure out what our next best step is. Taking time away from others and from our everyday lives is beneficial to our growth and it can act as another part of our internal GPS.

When we stop to breathe, we will never act out of haste. We will be able to learn to listen to what our intuition is trying to tell us. There are many ways in which to breathe: You can try meditation, exercise, yoga, music, a nap, soaking in the tub, going for a walk, a drive, etc. Whatever ways that help you to relax, shift your mental gears and breathe.

This week's assignment is another one that is short and sweet, yet to the point. When faced with rejection, a setback, a challenge of not knowing what to do, or of being overwhelmed, the best solution before you react is:

Stop! Breathe! Listen!

In the end, you will be glad that you did. One of the most helpful quotes that I have ever heard is one that I use the most and it applies to all things, "When you don't know what to do, don't do anything!"

This week practice your breathing. Learn to fit in a few seconds of breathing into your hectic schedule. Find a quiet space, close your eyes and focus on your breathing. I recommend using a 3-count. Breathe in to the count of 3, fill your lungs and hold to the count of 3 and exhale to the count of 3. Repeat as often as needed until you feel relaxed and breathe your way through your situations.

Weekly Affirmation:

I relax into the breath of life! I commend myself into this deep state of knowing and trust that all that I need to know will be revealed to me and through me. My breathing mantra is All Is Well.

My Thoughts

WORRY

Worry is wasted energy. We spend so much time worrying. We give a great deal of time worrying about things that never happen or about things that are out of our control. How many times have you worried about something and you got to the other side of the situation, only to find that your worry was wasted, and things turned out okay?

We must learn to release and to control our worry. Worry, if left to grow and prosper, will steal away your joy, peace and happiness. Goodness cannot get in if worry is standing in the way. Remember, what we focus on grows! When we let go of worry and the things and outcomes that we have no control over, then trust can take over and lead us to the right and best outcome. People talk so much about faith and trust, but when a challenge or a hardship presents itself, people tend to turn to fear and worry, instead of faith, hope and trust.

This week's message and lesson is short and sweet and can be hard to do. Can you let go of your need to control and not worry? Can you let go of your fear and worry and believe that someone or something greater than you will bring a right and perfect outcome? Can you practice letting go and letting the Universe take the lead in your life and know that all you need will show up for you?

Rest in this knowledge that what is meant for you will find you. What is meant to leave, let it go. What is meant to stay with you, will. And, some things are simply out of our control. Where can you practice this big, yet simple assignment in your life?

Weekly Affirmation:

I now trust... that what is meant to happen, will. I will choose not to worry, but to let go and surrender, so the best outcome will happen. I now choose to let someone greater than me do the worrying. I am at peace! I choose peace!

My Thoughts

RE-DEDICATION

Re-dedicate yourself to your intention. The resolutions, hopes, dreams and plans that were made back at the beginning of the year, how are they going? Are you still focused on them, or have you given up and gone back into your "normal" routine? Did it get too hard, or did you meet an obstacle and your fear shut it down?

Sometimes, we must show the Universe that we mean business and keep pushing forward. Maybe we need to pay attention to signs and omens that are showing up to guide us. Maybe, we got in our own way, wanting things on our watch and it didn't happen fast enough for us, so we gave up. Maybe we said, what's the use? Maybe we failed or got a rejection and we made an agreement with it.

When you want something, you must want it bad! More than anything!! Your determination will decide the outcome that you want. Never let anyone's No, be YOUR Yes! Do you know how many people are turned down, but they never gave up? They believed in themselves and their talent and they kept going until someone gave them a chance. Remember... a rejection is sometimes merely a redirection to put us on a better path or done for our best interests.

This week re-examine your goals and plans. Did you give up too easily, or are you still committed to making it happen? Have that heart to heart with yourself and re-dedicate yourself to your purpose. Pay attention to messages that show up guiding you closer to your intention. You can do this. I believe in you!

Weekly Affirmation:

I am re-dedicating myself to my dream. I believe in myself and I trust the Universe to help guide me along. Whenever I take a step, the Universe takes two more for me. I am now living my dream.

My Thoughts

MUSIC

Music is one of the great Healers and Teachers. It inspires and moves us like nothing else. The melody or words cause us to act in our lives and in our emotions. Lyrics can inspire us, or they can cause self-inflicted pain and suffering. What melody do you have playing in your life? Is it one of joy, peace, love and happiness? Or, is it one of pain, sadness, fear and lost hope?

Music and what we listen to, or sing along with, are like prayers that the Universe hears and answers. The Universe listens to every thought, every word, every song and confirms those things into our lives. Ask yourself, is what I am listening to creating the life that I want to see? Do you want more of the same? Or, something better? The choices are up to us. Music is sowing the seeds in our mental and emotional gardens, producing the fruit and vegetation that we plant.

What are you listening to? What are you humming? What song theme do you have playing in your mind? If it isn't happy or joyful, get rid of it! We can use music to inspire us, drive us and to heal the broken parts of us that need healing.

This week pay attention to the music choices that you are making. Do you want a life song of courage, power and strength? Or, a song of sorrow, defeat and failed love? If you don't like the music of your life... change the tape! If we are to pull to us the things that we desire, we must change the song that we sing.

Weekly Affirmation:

I now sing a new song! I only sing songs of hope, joy and peace. I create the melody that runs through my life, I now only listen to the beautiful song of hope and victory!

My Thoughts

STRENGTH

Imagine if you will, a Lion. What does a Lion represent to you? For me, a Lion represents, strength, courage, fierceness, loyalty and power. He is the king of the jungle. That same fierceness resides in you. The time has come for you to tap into that power source. The knowledge that whatever comes your way, you can handle it. The strength that you need is always available to you.

With strength, comes compassion. It is the flipside of strength, but the underbelly in which gentleness lives. Your strength and courage live in that compassionate part of you. It is where you may feel defeated, but it also is where you gather your power. You must be compassionate enough to love yourself through what you are facing and be determined to fiercely face what you are moving through.

That determination, gets you out of bed in the morning, helps you to put your crown on your head and move throughout your day in a victorious mindset.

This week, can you tap into the energy of the Lion and use it to conquer your weaknesses? Will you be The King or Queen of your jungle? Will you choose to defeat or to be defeated? The choice is up to you. Make a list of all the ways that you surrender your power and then, list how you can change that belief and tap into your power source.

Weekly Affirmation:

"I am Woman, hear me roar!" I am strong now and I am confident. I take back my power!

My Thoughts

_____

_____

_____

_____

_____

_____

_____

_____

_____

_____

_____

_____

PROUD

There is a song that poses the question, what have you done today to make you feel proud? Have you done something lately for yourself? Have you taken a step towards a better you? We all want others to be proud of us, but are you proud of who you are?

It is never too late to make this a reality. We put our happiness on hold to please someone else. We never take enough time to give back to ourselves and for that, we suffer. We often suffer and are so used to it that we don't even realize that we are suffering. We fall asleep in our pain and it can make us numb to realizing how we are living. The first step in self-care is knowing that you are important. If you don't take care of you, how can you give to someone else? What are things that make you happy? No matter how small they may seem, what are ways that you can give to you? Small steps lead to bigger steps and bigger steps cause achievement and that makes you feel proud! The more that you accomplish in your goals for you, the more excited you will feel. You are important and you matter, too. Your dreams, goals and visions for your life matter. You deserve to make them come true.

This week look at the areas in which you give too much of your Self away. Are there areas, places, people that you can change to be more giving to yourself? What can you do this week to make you feel proud? You deserve this. Your new life and self-esteem needs you. So, carve out some time and look for ways to accomplish some steps towards making you feel better about yourself. Remember, putting yourself first is not being selfish, it is being self-Full.

Weekly Affirmation:

I MATTER! I do today what makes me feel proud of who I am. I am living my dreams and I do what is needed to make myself feel good.

My Thoughts

Autumn

THE FALL

Seasons change and so do we. It is so funny and ironic how metaphorical our lives really are. We grow and age just like seasons and all things in nature. Our relationships grow and change, some mature and last, while others die off for new ones to begin. Fall is the colorful reminder that our seasons of life change and if seen, can morph into something more beautiful than we could even imagine. Our relationships, like seasons, ebb and flow and if closely examined, show us how they endure. Our relationships go through three stages. They last for a reason, a season or a lifetime and when each season ends, they end. In each one of these seasons, when the lesson has been learned and it has taught us all that we need to know, the season must end. If we try to hang on to what is over, it is only going to hurt us more.

Fall is a good time to turn to serious contemplation about life. To closely examine its meaning and a time to figure out what in your life needs to change. The array of colors in the Fall show us the beauty of life and the promise that life is ever changing. Just because something changes, something of great magnificence is possible. This is a great time to look at your life and to see if you are changing with each season. Is there enough color in your life? What needs to be let go of and what needs to stay? Can you trust the cycle of life and allow the seasons of your life and relationships to change and move into their best outcome? Are you willing to let Nature take its course and allow the dying process of things to happen and have faith that something more beautiful will grow? One of my favorite sayings is, "Let it go, because something beautiful wants to grow there!"

This week examine your heart and where you are in your seasons of life. What needs to go and what can stay? Don't be afraid of change. Spring will always come again.

Weekly Affirmation:

I trust the seasons of my life. As my seasons change, so do I and I change for the better. I trust that when something ends, something even better will come.

My Thoughts

FIRE

Have you gone back to sleep in your life? Have you lost your passion? Have you given up? Feel useless?

These things are necessary and part of manifesting your goals. They come to show us what we are made of. They teach us about perseverance and pushing through and the lessons of hope, faith and trust. We all need a break from time to time and that is perfectly okay. Just don't lose your vision for your life. You are needed to keep your fire going. What you desire is obtainable, you must want it. So, when you are feeling down, without any passion, or like a break is necessary, allow yourself to experience those feelings, but get back up as soon as possible. The challenge is to find what you can do to re-ignite your passion.

What can you do? What are things and ways to make you passionate again? We have already explored before that there are things that you can apply to help you through. Things like reading books, music, meditation, exercise, taking a class or workshop and if all of this fails... practice gratitude. The more that we show gratitude for what we have, the more that we increase that energy. When we give thanks for what we have, we will receive even more.

This week, where can you light a fire under your butt? I know that you do not want to stay where you are! Where can you turn to fan the flames of your life? This week spend some time with you. Have a heart to heart with yourself and discover ways to get back on track. Find and journal ways to re-ignite your life. You may not smoke, but I want you to re-start the fire for your heart's desire!

Weekly Affirmation:

I am passionate for life! I love life and life loves me! I am on fire to not settle for less than I deserve. Watch me burn!

My Thoughts

_____

_____

_____

_____

_____

_____

_____

_____

_____

_____

_____

_____

_____

FOCUS

Where is your focus? Where do you place your energy? Is it on love or fear? Is it a focus of hope or of despair? Can you believe that things can be different? Can you believe that things do not have to continue in the same old way? Do you want a better life? A life that is more peaceful, calm, content and happy? Do you believe that is it possible?

If you said yes to any of these questions, then they are possible. The sheer fact that you said yes, or that you want a better life, is a start. We may know how to achieve it and we may not. What matters most is you are willing to move in that direction.

So how do we get started? We begin to shift our perception and place our trust in the possibility that things can and will be better. We stop watering our garden of fear, defeat and hopelessness. We stop functioning from a victimized and defeated mentality. We can ask for help, support and guidance from our Source and ask to be shown a different way or better way. Once we ask, we can find pictures or words that show or describe what it is that we want to bring into our life and place them where we will see them. We can ask that the right and perfect people and things begin to show up that will lead us to a brighter future. We can ask that we recognize them when they show up and that we don't pass them by. We become determined and disciplined that we will start sowing the seeds of Hope, Promise and Victory, and let the field of lack, defeat and failure die off. We can stay in whatever place that we choose, and that choice is up to us. Do you want to overcome or to be overcome? Where do you wish to place your focus? Your dreams begin in the knowing that you can have your heart's desire.

This week pay attention and focus on your thoughts. Are they good or bad? Are they victorious or are they seeded in defeat? Work on turning them around and ask for the knowledge to do that. Write out the ways that you sabotage yourself and write out ways that you can conquer your patterns and how to turn your life and dreams around, making them a reality, not just a dream.

Weekly Affirmation:

Every thought that I think is creating my future. I choose thoughts of great success and purpose. I am now living the life of my dreams. I am victorious in all that I say and do!

My Thoughts

THE LIES

When we are all born, we come into the world like a blank tape. We have no opinion about the world and the way it is or how it is supposed to be. We are taught the things that we should think, what to believe, what to fear or who we are to grow up to be. Without our knowing, we accept these things as our truth and we grow up fearing and believing those things that were inflicted upon us. Our liberation comes if we have the wisdom to think for ourselves and to choose differently.

You are not the lies that others have forced upon you. You are a free spirit and you get to decide what is right and best for you. This is your life and no one else's! Yes, others have the right to say whatever they want to about us, but only we can give it power. If something doesn't feel right or doesn't make you feel empowered, choose again. Who you are matters and you have the right and freedom to choose what is best for you.

You are important, special and most of all, you matter! You get to decide how and where you will go in life. When you realize that others cannot control you, you are on your way to finding your truth. There will be others when you move out of "their" comfort zone who will try to dissuade you from doing what you want. They will try to make you feel wrong or like you will fail if you move outside of "the norm." But, you are on the right track and you keep going! Your greatness is depending on you. You are enough... keep going and trusting your faith and belief in yourself.

This week think about where you have surrendered your power. What were you told that you no longer believe? How can you stand up to your fears and start to believe that you are worthy of having the life that you want? Your positive beliefs will open the doorway to positive outcomes. Don't believe the lies!

Weekly Affirmation:

I AM A FREE SPIRIT! I am free to be me! My life, My choices!

My Thoughts

THE GOOD

How do we attract more good into our lives? We do that by appreciating and giving thanks for what we already have. Gratitude releases the power to bring more good into our lives. What we focus on, we create.

We should make a daily practice of finding the good in our everyday life. When we become more optimistic about situations in our lives, we shift the energy from the problem onto finding the solution or bright spot in them. This shift in perspective helps us to find the good that we need to be looking for.

Good happens around us all the time, we just allow the outside world to trick us into thinking that nothing good ever happens. Fear and chasing after what we want will cause the thing(s) of our attraction to run in the opposite direction, but when we send out thoughts and expressions of what we are grateful for and what we have, we will attract more good into our lives. We need to learn to appreciate more of the good that life has to offer and that increase in vibration will help to do so.

This week train your mind to seek out the good in everyday life. Start by shifting your perspective and outlook from the negative onto the possibilities in your situations. Remember... the more "Thanks" that you give, the more "Good" that you will find. Shift your perspective and change the way that you see things.

Weekly Affirmation:

I am surrounded by good. My good comes to me from all directions. Life loves me and supports me. I attract more good into my life. Bad can't get in the way, because there is so much good happening in my life!

My Thoughts

LIGHT

This week we are exploring The Light, your God center and expression in the world around you. Are you sharing your light with others? Can others see The Light shining from within you? Is your light bright, filled with love and hope? Is your light dull and unlit because of fear?

Your inner light is your God light. It is the center of who you are and who you should be. When your light is dull it projects more darkness into your life and out into your world. The world in which we live needs light. There is so much darkness in the world around us and it needs our light to illuminate a brighter way. We spend so much time allowing things to take away our light. It is time that we turn off the news and focus on finding or being the Good that we wish to see.

How can you share your light with the world this week? First off, make "God" or whatever you wish to call Him/Her, the center of your life. I have found that when I do not keep "God" as the center of my life... it simply does not work right. Second, turn off the news, radio, Internet, television, music, friends and family that keep you down and depressed. Feed your Soul with good things and knowledge and leave the rest behind. If it does not make you feel good or it takes away your joy, leave it alone. Start to take a stand and do not allow people or things to steal away your peace and happiness. Do only what increases happiness into your life and helps you to be more positive and in that place... you will find your Light!

Your life and your "Light" are needed! You have something special and unique to share with the world. We need you! This week ask Source to bring their Light into your life, so that you can share this Light with others. When you share your Light, it will increase the amount of Light that you receive in return.

Weekly Affirmation:

I AM the Light of the world! I share my Light wherever I go. Others see my Light shining in me and I see the Light reflected in all that I see. I AM a Beacon of Light!

My Thoughts

KARMA

Karma is one of the primary Universal Laws. It is the one that states whatever you put out will be returned to you. It is also referred to as Cause and Effect. There cannot be an effect without a cause. The Universe will deliver and return to us what we rightfully deserve. It does not edit, it does not know when we are joking, it serves us what we request and believe, so... watch your thoughts, words and actions. Learn to carefully watch what you say, what you put out into the world.

Karma not only delivers the bad, it delivers the good as well. Karma is the Server in the restaurant who brings to you what you ask for. Monitor your selections carefully. Do not be surprised when the dish is served and do not be shocked at the bill! With Karma, payment is always due. When dealing with the Laws of Karma, will you sow good things, or will you sow negative? Will you choose to live in peace, or will you continue to be angry, mad, hurt, rejected and spew those things out into your world? We cannot have a negative mind and expect good things to show up! We must tend to the field of our thoughts and beliefs. If we expect a good harvest, we must choose carefully what we plant.

Karma is one of the biggest teachers of life. She quietly observes what we do and in due time, serves her justice. Yes, bad things happen to good people and no one will get out of here without having bad things and times happen.

This week make sure that what you put out doesn't come back to bite you in the butt! Let go of anger and resentments quickly and practice forgiveness often because... everything you do, comes back to you. EVERYTHING!

Weekly Affirmation:

I now choose to forgive and let go of the things and people that no longer serve me. I choose love and only my good is returned to me. I plant only good seeds.

My Thoughts

THANKSGIVING

What are you grateful for? Have you stopped along the way to say Thank You? For some people, it takes a holiday like Thanksgiving to turn their hearts and minds toward gratitude. We should live in a constant state of thanksgiving. We should not wait for the holidays to roll around to be grateful for what we have. Thanksgiving should be a continual and committed offering that we do to show our appreciation for all that we have. Do you wait until you get what you want to offer your thanks? Even during times of dis-ease, we can find ways to offer our thanks. We may have to look a bit harder to find gratitude, but it is always there.

When we express and show our gratitude, it activates the principles of attraction of receiving more blessings into our life. The Laws of Attraction, Karma and Cause and Effect all carry the same message. What you give out shall be returned! What you sow, so shall you reap!

When we keep our thoughts and vibrations focused and appreciative on the good in our life, it will open the path for more good to come into our lives. That is why thanksgiving and gratitude are so important. We are paving the way for something better to come into our life.

The past brought us to where we are today, it was necessary and had to happen... bless it. Now, let's change our focus onto today and live a life of purposeful thanksgiving. Our future depends on us: What we believe, we will see. May you be blessed this Thanksgiving, and may your Heart forever live in gratitude.

Weekly Affirmation:

Thank you, God for everything! For all that I have and for all that I receive, I say THANK YOU!!

My Thoughts

_____

_____

_____

_____

_____

_____

_____

_____

_____

_____

_____

_____

_____

CONFUSION

Sometimes, the way is not clear. In those moments, we need to trust the process. When the way is not clear, we need to take that time to pause and to reflect on where we have been and a possible new way of getting to where we want to go. Confusion does not necessarily have to be confusing. It can simply be a time when we take a break and let The Divine take the lead. Maybe we are in our own way? Maybe we are being re-directed for our own good? Maybe the confusion has come to protect us from making a mistake? Whatever the reason, confusion can be our friend.

We need to trust our processes of life and in creating the things that we want. When we take a break or rest and get out of own way, the Universe will work out the details that are needed. Maybe the opportunity isn't available yet. When I was shopping for my current house, I had looked at over 50 houses. I was exhausted in the process, but I stayed committed to what I exactly wanted in my next home. When it looked like my house wasn't out there, I stopped looking. A week later, my Realtor called and said a house was being listed the next day. I was the first one in to see it and the house was IT! So, my confusion in the process showed me that my house was not currently available, but when it was ready, the way was shown.

This week, if you are confused in your life situations, take that much needed pause, ask for patience and further investigation and relax in the knowledge that when the time is made perfect, your next steps will be made known. Rely on the comfort of your weekly affirmation and write your way through this confusing timeframe.

Weekly Affirmation:

What is meant for me, will always find me. What I need will always be supplied. There is no need for me to worry. Worry is wasted energy. Instead, I choose peace.

My Thoughts

RENEWAL

Renewal: A time to dust off what is old and start anew. The dormant time is now complete, it is time to step into being a better you. You have beat yourself up, put yourself down, made yourself feel "less than" and now it is time to manifest a better version of who you are. In case no one has told you, let me be the first: YOU MATTER! You matter!! You always have. I searched my whole life for someone to say that to me and when I was open and receptive to it, I heard those words and I received them. It changed me for the better. Can you hear and receive those words today? You Matter. I hope that you can.

And... how you show up in all things matter! Even when running errands or going to the grocery store, how you show up matters! We must set the tone for what we want to be in the world! What do you want the world to see? How will you show the world that you deserve to be taken seriously and that you mean business? What "drag" will you put on to show a new and improved you? Remember... if the inside is ugly, it won't matter what the outside looks like. So, work on the interior part of yourself and know that who you are matters. Raise your head high and walk like you are worthy. I have always heard that your confidence enters the room before you do! Own it. This week, I want you to know how important you are. That you are valuable, lovable and so worth loving. You are needed in the world! We need your light. How will you show up in the world? Because... how you show up, is what you will receive in return!

This week, how can you show the world who you really are? Work on knowing that you are enough! Tell yourself the things that you are longing to hear from someone else. How can you be or give those things to you? That is where it must start, with you! Dress for success. Dress how you want the world to see you. And, BE the love that you wish to see.

Weekly Affirmation:

I MATTER! I now love WHO I AM, and I AM WORTH LOVING! I attract all the good that I put out into the world. I AM BEAUTIFUL, IMPORTANT and I MATTER!!

My Thoughts

JUMP

Are you ready to take that leap of faith? Are you tired of doing the same old thing and getting the same result? Is there a calling that you haven't answered? Is fear of failing standing in your way?

If you answered yes to any of these questions, then your life is speaking to you. But, are you listening? Jumping means to be brave and daring, to leap fully into your life and go after your dreams. It is about being fully in your power and doing what is right and best for you. It means putting yourself first for a change, so that there can be change. Most of the time we must pursue our dreams. We must be brave and take the first step needed to make them happen. When we do... The Universe will begin to show us the next step to take. The things that you want are waiting on you! Are you going to keep them a dream, or make them a reality? We spend too much time and energy letting things hold us back. We waste precious time allowing others to stand in our way, not believing in ourselves and letting fear run our emotions. I have often heard that, "the thing that you fear is the very thing that you should be doing."

So, where this week can you jump and take charge of your life? What are you allowing to hold you back? What or who do you need to let go of so that you can have the life that you want? This week take the time to ready yourself and to make yourself strong enough to jump! Your life is waiting for you!! You might ask yourself, what if I fail? But, I ask you... what if you fly? The longer that you wait, the more valuable time is wasted.

This week do one thing every day that you fear. If there are blocks, write and journal about them. Do a close examination and be extremely honest about why you are afraid of following your goal.

Weekly Affirmation:

I am now brave and confident enough to JUMP into my life. I am now living the life of my dreams. I am no longer afraid! This is MY life and I am taking charge of it. Life loves me and supports me. I have all that I need to be a success.

My Thoughts

_____

_____

_____

_____

_____

_____

_____

_____

_____

_____

_____

_____

_____

IMAGINATION

As soon as you can, sit somewhere quietly and close your eyes and allow yourself to dream and imagine what it would look like to be living your perfect life. Describe it in detail and be daring enough to dream big. What would you be doing? Where would you be? We all have visions for our future, but how can we turn them into a reality?

As children, we were always daydreaming and pretending to be someone or somewhere else, our imaginations would run wild. We need to find that child-like quality again. Indulge in the wonderment of dreams and the courage to chase after them.

What can you do to spark that creative juice to make it flow again? First, you can sit and daydream about what it is that you want to bring more of into your life. Ask yourself, what do I want for my life? What would that look like? How can I achieve it? What can I do to ignite the imagination that I need to go after my dreams? What inspires you? The answers to these questions can be found in your imagination. To dream the impossible dream is one thing, but to go after it is another. This week, I want you to explore your imagination. I want you to get excited about allowing yourself to imagine and to dream again. It does not matter how big or small, dream and give yourself permission to play in your imagination. In order for a dream to be achieved, it must first be conceived, and that conception happens in your wildest imagination. Know, trust and believe, that all things are possible. Walt Disney wished upon a star and look what happened to him! The same can happen for you.

Weekly Affirmation:

I give myself permission to let my imagination run free. I know and trust that the Universe can dream a bigger dream for me than I can even imagine. I am open and receptive to all the good that is coming my way.

My Thoughts

ACCEPTANCE

This week we are discussing the acceptance of acceptance. Acceptance of the way that things are going or the way that things have turned out. Acceptance is NOT failure! It is merely the understanding that things have turned out the way that they were supposed to be. Acceptance does not mean defeat! It means that we accept what has happened or what had to happen and begin the process of moving forward in a new direction. Remember... what looks like a "setback" is the catalyst to take you where you are supposed to go.

Acceptance is one of the final steps in the grieving process. When we lose someone to death or divorce, when someone chooses to leave our life, when we don't get that job or the house we wanted, when we are turned down or rejected, the time will come that we must accept what happened and trust that what is meant for us will find us.

The sooner that we can get to accepting the outcome in situations, the sooner we can move toward achieving success in what is really our destiny. Bad things happen. But, they come to teach us things that we needed to learn that we would not have learned any other way. Life is happening for us, not to us. As soon as we can recognize this principle, the quicker acceptance can take place.

This week, in what areas of your life do you need acceptance? Have you made peace from the broken pieces of your life? Have you forgiven everything and everyone so that you can be free to receive the best results that life is trying to send your way? Acceptance is the understanding that what happened was not an ending, but merely a friend that came to send you in a better direction.

Weekly Affirmation:

I am making peace from my broken pieces. I am at peace and trust that what is meant for me will always find me. I accept what had to happen and I peacefully move forward. The best is yet to come.

My Thoughts

_____

_____

_____

_____

_____

_____

_____

_____

_____

_____

_____

_____

_____

Winter

RESPONSIBILITY

Let me start by saying, YOU are responsible for your life!

As a source of energy, you are responsible for the energy that you bring into a room. You are also responsible for the energy that you allow to stay around you. Others are not always responsible with their energy and for what they bring with them so, it is your responsibility to protect your well-being, your life.

If others are not encouraging or supportive of where you are trying to take your life, then you may need to do some clearing out of who you allow to stay close to you. This can be hard to do. Sometimes this clearing means longtime friends, loved ones and family members that you must sever ties with if they are not a positive influence for you. You cannot move up in your life or where it is that you are trying to go if you allow people close to you who only keep you down.

As you change, the people around you must change. You must surround yourself with winners. People who have a positive outlook on life. People who are going somewhere with their life. Ones who are successful and who are inspiring. Not the ones who are nothing more than "Energy Suckers," who will suck the joy and energy out of your life.

This week take a good long look at the people in your life. Who is around you? Are they happy and supportive people? Do they inspire and encourage you? Do they lift you up or do they bring you down? Are they responsible with their life or are they full of drama and chaos? Where can you start to distance yourself from the Energy Suckers in your life? Do you believe that you are worth more? Do you want to achieve great success? Look closely, is it time to do some spring cleaning in your life and clear the space around you? Winners hang out with other winners!

Weekly Affirmation:

I take responsibility for my life and my energy! I am a magnet that attracts like- minded people to me. I am only going up! I am a magnet of only goodness.

My Thoughts

COMMITMENT

Are you committed to your life? Are you willing to commit to your purpose and to your heart's desire? We often jump into things without making sure that we are ready to commit. Whether it is a goal, job, pet or relationship, we must first be ready to make the commitment necessary for its success. With commitment comes determination. We need determination to ensure that what we want to make successful will succeed. There can be no intention without a commitment.

The tricky part of commitment is if you are unavailable, so will be your intention. In a relationship, if any part of us is unavailable, we will attract to us partners that are unavailable as well. Others mirror what we are internally feeling. We must be open, vulnerable and available to pull to us a lasting committed relationship. When we rush into them, without unpacking our emotional baggage, we will find ourselves unpacking from the last one in the present one. If we are not ready to commit to something, chances are it will not be a lasting situation.

So, are you ready to commit to your goal? Can you make the commitment to fulfill your dreams? Are you ready to make the agreement with yourself to giving all of you to whatever it is that you want to succeed? Commitment takes work. It takes courage and availability. It requires us to be 100% available to making it a success. In the past you may have been hurt or disappointed, but if we don't make the commitment to try again, we will never know the meaning of success.

This week, ask yourself... Am I ready and willing to commit? If so, go for it and make your dreams a reality. Take that chance! If you are not or unsure, more work is needed. Spend time uncovering your fears about commitment and do the work that is required. There are 3 levels of healing. We must first feel, so that we can deal to heal. Feel. Deal. Heal. Do your work and make yourself ready to commit. Your life is waiting on YOU!

Weekly Affirmation:

I am available to life! I commit myself fully to my life and I now make myself available for my dreams to come true. I am ready to commit!

My Thoughts

LIFE CLASS

Your life is like a classroom. You will find at times that you are both Student and Teacher. Life is the classroom in which we come to learn. Everyone and everything is our teacher. There is always something of value to be learned. One of the great principles of this Earth School is the assignment of lessons. We are all given the appropriate lessons that we need to help us learn the things that we need to know. It is our job to find out what these lessons are and to find out exactly what they come to teach us.

One of the toughest assignments is to master the lessons so they do not have to be repeated. This is another one of the great principles of Life Class: Lessons are repeated until learned. It has been said we do not have multiple relationships with different people, we repeat the same lesson with several different people. The same person continues to show up over and over, they just wear a different pair of pants. Our lesson is to see past their disguise and recognize them when they show up. Then, choose accordingly.

Life loves us so much that it brings to us the lessons that we need to learn to cause growth for our Soul. Life is really for us and not against us. We need to realize that the best students do get the hardest tests and that while we are here, learning never ends. Have you seen repeated lessons of learning in your life? Are there people that keep reappearing in your life that you recognize from before? Are you choosing not to see the lesson in something that needs to be learned? When something happens, can you train yourself to ask the big questions of why? Why did this happen? What has this come to teach me? What is it that I am supposed to be learning from this and what is it that I need to know? When we begin the process of answering these life test questions, we will discover the learning that is necessary for our graduation from the class called LIFE!

Weekly Affirmation:

My life is a class and I am successful in my learning. All that I need to know will be revealed at the right and perfect time. I am open to learning and I share what I know.

My Thoughts

THE MASK

One of the greatest teachings that I ever heard was, "When people show you who they are, believe them the first time." Dr. Maya Angelou was one of my favorite authors and teachers. Her wisdom, writing and teachings helped to shape the trajectory of my life. Those words of wisdom spoke volumes to my soul. All that I could think was, why didn't I hear that years ago? That knowledge would have saved me from many heartaches and spared me from people who were not good for me. I now know that they were meant for me and were lessons that I needed to go through to learn what I needed to know.

Do you listen carefully to what others tell you about themselves? Are you watching and observing their actions and what they are showing you? Actions DO speak louder than words. Have you ever gotten a "red flag" about someone, knowing that they would not be good for you and you continued to hang around with them and were later disappointed or hurt by them? If so, they showed you in the beginning, who they were, and you chose not to heed that warning. That is an example of someone showing you "who they were." People like to wear a mask of disguise and hide who they really are. Pay attention!

Being observant is one of the greatest tools that we have. It pays for us to pay attention and to be alert about what or who is around us. It is hard to remove someone from our life once they get in. If we are observant and learn to listen to our gut feelings about certain people or places, then we can be spared a lot of wasted time and energy.

This week pay attention to the people and things around you. Have you experienced in the past a time when someone showed you "who they were" and you ignored it? This week learn to notice what's going on around you and be observant to what the Universe is trying to show you.

Weekly Affirmation:

I am observant to my life. I am aware, and I pay attention to the subtle messages that others try to show me. I am aware now.

My Thoughts

MINDING YOUR BUSINESS

This week we are dealing with the subject of minding your business. A helpful quote that I heard was, "You do not have to participate in every fight that you are invited to." This means, if someone is trying to pick a fight with us or get us into an exchange with them and it doesn't feel good, we can choose not to get involved. One of the best things that we can do is to say nothing or as little as possible and walk away as soon as we can. We can learn to listen to others about their problems and learn to hand their issues back to them. Others, as well as ourselves, need to learn to fix our own problems. All of us are responsible for our lives and that includes our problems.

We have all heard the saying, "tend to your own backyard" and this implies that we need to tend to what is going on with us and stay out of other people's affairs. Why are we quick to judge others when our life is no better? The best thing we can do is to allow others to handle their problems and we handle our own. It is tempting to want to get involved, people like a good drama but... you might wish that you had stayed out of it. We all need to learn our own lessons. It is not our place to save someone, to fix someone or to try to take the learning away from someone. When you do this, you block the blessing of what the issue has come to teach them.

Lastly, be careful with whom you share your business. People like a good juicy story and if you are not careful, they will tell your business. Chances are, if they talk to you about someone else, they will probably talk about you. So, mind your business and let others mind theirs. No matter how hard it can be to stay out of the middle of someone else's affairs, DO IT! You might get hurt in the end.

This week, how can you find ways to mind your business? How can you be helpful to others and not get involved? Do you gossip? If so, look for ways to stop it.

Weekly Affirmation:

I allow others to learn their own lessons and I learn my own. I remain at peace and let others fix their own lives. I mind my business and others mind theirs.

My Thoughts

THE PAST

The past is over! Leave it there!!

The sooner that we can forgive the past, the sooner that we can move forward. As soon as you can, realize that everything that has happened had to happen to bring you to where you are today. The principle that life happens *for* us, not *to* us is important information needed to explain that life comes to teach us, not hurt us. We forgive the past and others, not to condone what they did, but to set ourselves free from the pain of the past.

There are valuable tools from the past that we can take with us on our journey towards our future. We can use them to help shape and mold our future into what we choose to see. We will no longer settle for how we lived in the past. Set it free! Our cars have rear view mirrors and like those mirrors, we can see where we've been, but they do not dictate where we are going. Stop looking backwards; we are not going that way!

Start this week—even better start right now—living in the present moment. Do not worry about your tomorrows; stay focused on the present moment. Choose to live in this second, then the next minute, the next hour and take things one day at a time. When we look at the big picture it can scare us into not doing what it is that we need to do. This week look for ways that you can leave your past behind. How can you do that? Focus on where you are today and where you want to be tomorrow. Follow your steps, one at a time that will lead you to following your bliss. The past is over! Thank God!!!

Weekly Affirmation:

I am now choosing to leave the past behind! My future is so bright, it blinds my eyes!! I live in The Now!!

My Thoughts

REBOOT

When you have done all that you can do, given all that you can give, maybe it is time for a re-boot, so to speak? Our minds are like a computer and sometimes we need to be unplugged for a clear way to begin. We all need time to stop and rewind, in order to move forward. Once again, a "pause" may be necessary.

We can become overwhelmed with life and all the stresses that are placed upon us and there comes a time when we simply need to disconnect and take care of us. When we are experiencing burn out, we cannot function on the level that is expected of us. Others will not receive our best if we are not fully charged.

The great thing about a re-boot is we can give ourselves permission to stop the world, go within and find what it is to make us feel whole again. We need to have time where we shut everything out and be alone to give back to us.

This week, what do you need? Do you need time alone? Do you need to turn off the world and rest? Do you need peace and relaxation? Can you carve out some time to give back to yourself and nurture your spirit? Most of all, do you need a re-boot to clear your mind of all the clutter that has accumulated? Give yourself permission to stop trying to do everything and be everything and let yourself unwind. You will be glad that you did, and you might even find what you have been looking for... YOU!

Weekly Affirmation:

I give myself time to re-charge. I love myself and I give myself permission to give back to me. I matter, and I now do what I need to do to give myself a break.

My Thoughts

LIBERATION

What does the word Liberation mean to you? For me, it means freedom, release, permission, courage and peace.

Where in your life do you need liberation? Is there something or someone that holds you back that you need a release from? We often stay too long in places that are comfortable to us. We stay in relationships and in places that we are familiar with and if we closely examine, are ones that are reflective of the environment of our childhood. We stay with, or attract to us, these things that we may need liberation from. We attract them to us, even if we did not like them, because we tend to repeat our patterns. We repeat these patterns for the teachings that they hold. We attract the same experiences and partners to us to move us toward our liberation of the past.

What do you need liberation from?

When I told my family the secret that I carried, I was liberated. I liberated myself! I liberated myself, not because I needed their approval, I did it for me and for my liberation. Secrets carry a lot of weight and responsibility with them. You cannot be fully liberated carrying that baggage. Baggage only weighs you down.

Isn't it time that you were free and liberated from that pressure?

This week work on your liberation! Where can you free yourself from the chains that hold you back? Where can you find your freedom to let go, so that you can let your heart run free? Love liberates. It releases and holds nothing back. This week let love liberate you, and in that healing may you find your peace of mind.

Weekly Affirmation:

I am free! I let love and liberation free my soul. I give myself permission to live my best life, the one that I deserve to live.

My Thoughts

HOPE

Hope, such a small word that carries amazing power and authority. When we are faced with endings and completions in our lives, it is easy to lose hope. Then, when we are facing times of promise and salvation, hope is renewed. Does hope ever really go away? Is it always there, like a silent friend, allowing us to fall and then catching us when we do?

Hope is like the sunrise after the darkest night. Hope is the Sun that shines after a storm. It comes to illuminate the way and brings the energy that things are going to be alright. It is the courage to tackle what life throws our way and it rallies us to believe in things that are unseen.

We lose faith and we lose hope, but I believe in my heart that they never disappear; we are the ones that choose not to see them. Just the same as God, hope never truly abandons us, it just lets us find our way until something shifts our pain.

One of the best affirmations that I ever received was and is: "Nothing is taken away unless something better is coming!" What a gift of promise and of hope that statement makes. A validation of whatever or whoever leaves our life, something better will come and take its place. In the redeeming quality of receiving that statement into your heart, there is hope. Yes, hope is always present and is always there to remind us that even though we must face our darkest times, hope will return to bring light to show us the way.

This week, work on bringing hope to whatever challenges you may be facing. Let go of what needs to go and use hope to truly HOPE for better days.

Weekly Affirmation:

I AM hopeful! I know that the worst is behind me and that better days are now here.

My Thoughts

_____

_____

_____

_____

_____

_____

_____

_____

_____

_____

_____

_____

GRACE

What is grace? To me, it is the silent beauty that underlies the receiving of our blessings. It is movement. It is form. It is the purest definition of unconditional love. Webster defines it as God's unmerited love for man. Grace is ease and simplicity. What I have come to know is there can be grace in all things.

The Universe/God is so good to us. It truly provides everything that we need. It even knows what is not for our highest good and through grace we are protected. I have come to understand in my life that what is meant for me will always find me. The things that we try to manifest or create should come to us in a graceful and easy way. In manifesting, if something does not come to us easily and effortlessly, we may need to consider that it may not be meant for us. Through the grace of God, we are protected for our highest good. Through grace, we can relax and trust that what is meant for us will indeed find us.

Grace like gratitude is a thanksgiving for what we are blessed to receive. Grace always knows what is best for us. Can you trust this process? We sometimes are not given what we want, but through the grace of God and the Universe, we are given what we need.

This week pay attention to where grace shows up in your life. Remember that grace is a silent and easy movement that looks out for our best interests. As you move gracefully through your days ahead, give thanks for your blessings received and trust that grace will guide you gently to your greatest good. Grace is the most beautiful of Angels, she moves quietly and unconditionally through our lives, bringing to us our highest good. Give thanks for this precious gift.

Weekly Affirmation:

All things move with grace and ease in my life. I trust the processes of Life and know that grace will always deliver what is meant for me. I believe that all is well.

My Thoughts

MAGIC

Do you believe in magic? Can you trust in unseen forces that are here to help and assist you? Do you practice faith? Because faith is a practice. It is the belief in the things that are unseen. With faith comes trust. They are loving sisters that work together to bring about our highest good. Whether you believe in Angels, Guides, or other heavenly beings, tap into the belief that someone is there, hearing your prayers and delivering them to the right and perfect Source to bring them to you. Now Grace, is the other sister. She carries our hopes and dreams and brings them to us. She is a silent worker. She is quiet, yet strong, loving and supportive, knowing that what is meant for us will be provided.

Magic is power! It is the fuel that is needed to bring your dreams to life. It is a ritual of sorts, that births your wildest visions and gently brings them forth. Without magic, there is no possibility. We must believe in the unseen magic forces to manifest our dreams.

This week, can you believe and trust in the power of magic? Can you surrender your deepest secrets to it and use its power for your greatest good? Our Muses want to help and assist us, but WE must ask for their assistance.

Use them this week to bring all your dreams alive for you.

Weekly Affirmation:

I trust in the power of Magic! I believe that all that I desire is coming to me now! I release all fear and doubt and know that unseen forces are guiding my every step, and all will be made clear in divine time and order.

My Thoughts

MIRACLE

I love Christmas! I always have, and I guess that I always will. I don't enjoy the pressures of Christmas or the commercialism of the holidays. I love what Christmas stands for or what it should, the magic and wonder of what it brings. The offering of fellowship and expressions of love that are ours to give and to receive. The miracles that are present and the hope of better things to come and the silent night of peace, joy and happiness.

There is hope and there are miracles available to us throughout the year, not only at the holidays. We receive the gift of life daily and it is up to us to be grateful for all that we have. We may not always like what we are given or where we are in life, but there is always hope for a better tomorrow. That same hope and gratefulness is at the heart of the miracle called Life.

Christmas heralds the hope of miracles to come. The promise that things can be better and that through the love and birth of the Christ, we are loved and that we can be that expression. What we give out in life shall be returned. If we are to truly expect a miracle we must believe and surrender that it can happen. When we are faced with a challenge in life, we should ask, in prayer, for a "miracle" in the situation. When we ask for a miracle, we need to let go of our control of how we think it should be answered and let The Divine take the lead. We should ask that the miracle be for the right and perfect outcome for ALL that are involved, and that Divine Time and Order be in place. This is true letting go.

Miracles can and do happen. There is always a child-like wonder that comes with the holiday season. It is up to us to try to find it and release it to share with others and the world around us. How can you be that expression? How can you BE what you wish to see? Can you believe in miracles and the hope that things are perfect, even when they are not in perfect order? Be love and give love, so that you will receive the greatest gift of all, the one of being truly loved.

Weekly Affirmation:

I believe in Miracles! I not only believe, but I expect one to happen whenever I need one. Thank you for the gift and hope of miracles.

My Thoughts

YOUR SACRED JOURNEY

We are at the end of another year and what a year it has been! I hope that as you close out one year and move into a new one, that you look back fondly at the year we are leaving behind and look boldly into the new one that is upon us. I hope that you know where it is that you are going to, and I hope that you are ready to blaze purposefully into your future.

Throughout the writings of this book, I hope that the message received from me to you is, YOU MATTER! Who you are matters and with that knowing and acceptance, you can achieve your wildest dreams. I want you to know and believe that you are made of greatness. Set your intention high and never settle for less than your heart's desire.

If I can leave you with one last pearl of wisdom, it would be keep your focus on your intention clear and try your best to not send out mixed messages to the Universe. That way, you will receive exactly what it is that you are trying to bring into your life and there will be no confusion or mayhem with it. To do that, keep your self-worth and esteem high and know that you deserve to have what you are looking to achieve.

In closing, always remember... this is YOUR life! No one else gets to decide what is best for you. Your journey is very sacred and only you can take it. The journey can be challenging from time to time. But, that is what makes the journey beautiful and worthwhile. The journey is about the "valley" that we must sometimes go through for learning to take place. Be brave and dare to walk alone if you must and to discover who you are and what it is that you want.

Look back in appreciation and look forward to the possibilities that await you in the new year. Your dreams and goals are waiting for you. Go get them! I am sending the happiest of intentions to you. May all your wishes come true.

Weekly/Yearly Affirmation:

As I anticipate the New Year and I ask what is coming for me I say, "Only the best is coming. The very best that life and love have to bring me!" All is well.

My Thoughts

CONCLUSION

Our life is a very sacred journey, one that we must take on our own. We are the ones responsible for the outcome of our life. We are the ones who get to choose what is right and best for us. We no longer need to sit on the sidelines and watch the world go by. We can be bold and daring and step up and play the game called Life. We can trust the process of letting go when necessary and trust that when things are meant for us, they will find us. In manifesting the life that we desire, we must always remember that what is meant for us will find us. We must know that what we need will always be there and our needs will always be met.

Just like the ever-changing seasons of nature, our lives go through change. We grow and evolve on our journey in life. We must learn to grow through our changes if we are to become what we wish to be. We must be brave to "go it alone" if necessary, to become who we are meant to be. We must learn the artful practice of letting go, to surrender our hopes and dreams to the Source that is greater than us and to believe that we are deserving of all good things. Like the seasons of change in nature, people and things die away in our life, but they are replaced with new things and better people who support the vision that we are creating for ourselves. It is never easy to say goodbye to ones who have meant so much, but we must learn to say goodbye.

There is power in letting go and in endings. It is the endings that bring the new beginnings that take us to where we are meant to be. Our lives begin at the end of our comfort zones and we can trust in that process. We must be brave enough to take the leap of faith when it is presented if we are to jump into the life of our dreams. I believe that when we take the first step in claiming our happiness, the Universe will take the next steps for us.

Stay awake in your life. Pay attention to the signs when they show up and use them as your guide. When we practice this awareness, we will be led to where we are meant to go. Your life is your responsibility. What you make of it is up to you! Remember, the Universe can dream a bigger dream for us than we can ever imagine. Let the dreaming begin and good luck! Most of all, thank you for your support. Happy manifesting!

P.S.

Like the great sleuth and homicide detective Columbo would say, "Just one more thing!"

Don't forget to set a deadline to whatever it is that you are creating. Deadlines give power and structure. They also give accountability to the achievement of your dreams. Without them we tend to keep things in the future tense, rather than taking the action needed to make them happen. Deadlines help to keep us true to our word and make us complete a task. Deadlines help. Deadlines work!

Affirming Affirmation:

I confidently take the needed action to make my dreams come true. Like any great story, I give them power and authority by creating a beginning, middle and end. I trust in the knowing, that when something ends, something new begins.

ABOUT THE AUTHOR

While enjoying a successful, 30-year career as a salon owner, Eddie tapped into his other passion, Metaphysics, in 1996. He is the owner/founder of Wolf Moon, LLC, a company designed for the learning and continuing education of Spirituality and Self-growth.

Eddie has helped transform the exteriors of thousands of people throughout his career as a stylist, but his true joy is achieving inner transformation for his clients through private intuitive sessions. In addition to being a serious student of Metaphysics for over 20 years, he teaches meditation, is a writer for Odyssey (a spiritual publication), is a licensed Reiki Practitioner and has received achievement in the field of Psychic Development. Self-help and motivational work are his passions and helping others achieve their dreams his goal.

Eddie resides in Louisville, KY., with his Life Companion and their dog, Princess.

Connect with Eddie: Eddie@EddieStratton.com

ACKNOWLEDGEMENTS

I am beyond excited about the publishing of my first book. There are so many people to thank, who without their help, none of this would be possible.

First, I must thank God and His/Her Universe for all things that are possible.

Many thanks to my writing coach and dear friend, Barbara Grassey and my longtime friend Sharon Vornholt. Without your vision and guidance, none of this would have been possible.

Thanks to my parents, who love me unconditionally and who have always been my biggest fans. Most of all, thanks to my Mom, who continues to affect and direct my life from the other side. I love and miss you daily.

To my family and friends, know that I love each one of you. Without you, I am nothing!

To my first teacher, who showed up when I called for help, Dee Patterson, thank you! You helped save me.

I would like to thank David Green for his gorgeous cover design; Shannon Casey, photographer extraordinaire, for making me look good; Kevin Bayless for a kick-ass logo; and Linda L. Barton for the interior layout.

To Jeff, you were gone too soon. You changed everything!

To Life, you have been the classroom that I have loved and hated, but you have made me into who I am today. Thank you for the lessons.

Lastly, to my Packy, you are my everything! You help to make the rest of my life, the best of my life and for that I am so grateful. I love you. Thank you for going up this staircase with me.

To my readers, thank you for taking this journey and know that you are responsible for your life. What you make of it is up to you. I hope that I have presented information to help your wildest dreams come true.

Peace and Blessings!

Made in the USA
Middletown, DE
17 July 2018